Pebble®
Plus

GREAT ASIAN AMERICANS

# Tammy Duckworth

by Stephanie Cham

CAPSTONE PRESS
a capstone imprint

Pebble Plus is published by Capstone Press,
1710 Roe Crest Drive, North Mankato, Minnesota 56003
www.mycapstone.com

**Library of Congress Cataloging-in-Publication Data**
Names: Cham, Stephanie, author.
Title: Tammy Duckworth / by Stephanie Cham.
Description: North Mankato, Minnesota : Capstone Press, 2018.
Series: Pebble plus. Great Asian Americans
Identifiers: LCCN 2017044059 (print) | LCCN 2017046525 (ebook) | ISBN 9781515799764
  (eBook PDF) | ISBN 9781515799559 (hardcover) | ISBN  9781515799702 (pbk.)
Subjects: LCSH: Duckworth, Tammy, 1968—Juvenile literature. | Women legislators—
  United States—Biography—Juvenile literature. | Legislators—United States—Biography—
  Juvenile literature. | United States. Congress. Senate--Biography—Juvenile literature. |
  Women politicians—United States--Biography—Juvenile literature. | Thai Americans—
  Illinois—Chicago--Biography—Juvenile literature. | Illinois. General Assembly. House of
  Representatives—Biography—Juvenile literature.
Classification: LCC E840.8.D83 (ebook) | LCC E840.8.D83 C47 2018 (print) |
  DDC 328.73/092 [B] –dc23
LC record available at https://lccn.loc.gov/2017044059

**Editorial Credits**
Abby Colich, editor; Juliette Peters and Charmaine Whitman, designers;
Morgan Walters, media researcher; Kathy McColley, production specialist

**Photo Credits**
Getty Images: Aaron P. Bernstein, 21, Chris Maddaloni, Cover, David S. Holloway, 13, Paul
Morigi, 17; Newscom: CHIP SOMODEVILLA/REUTERS, 9, DAVID CARSON/KRT, 15,
Douliery Olivier/ABACA USA, 5, JASON REED/REUTERS, 19; Shutterstock: Attitude, design
element throughout, j avarman, (pattern) design element throughout, most popular, design
element throughout, Roman Babakin, 7, VanderWolf Images, 11

## Note to Parents and Teachers

The Great Asian Americans set supports standards related to biographies.
This book describes and illustrates the life of Tammy Duckworth. The images
support early readers in understanding the text. The repetition of words
and phrases helps early readers learn new words. This book also introduces
early readers to subject-specific vocabulary words, which are defined in the
Glossary section. Early readers may need assistance to read some words and
to use the Table of Contents, Glossary, Read More, Internet Sites, Critical
Thinking Questions, and Index sections of the book.

Printed and bound in the USA.
010771S18

# Table of Contents

# Early Life

Tammy Duckworth was born in 1968. She had one brother. Her mother was Thai and Chinese. Her father was American. The family moved around Asia for his job.

**1968**
born on March 12 in Bangkok, Thailand

In 1984 Tammy's family moved to Hawaii. Soon she went to college. She joined ROTC. ROTC helps students get ready for the military.

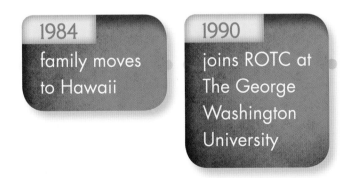

1984
family moves to Hawaii

1990
joins ROTC at The George Washington University

1968

THE
GEORGE
WASHINGTON
UNIVERSITY

FOUNDED
1821

# Flying for the Army

Tammy went to U.S. Army flight school in 1993. She became a helicopter pilot. She was the only woman in her unit.

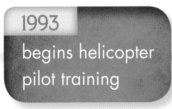

1993
begins helicopter pilot training

1968    1984    1990

The Iraq War began in 2003.

Tammy went to fight.

Her helicopter was attacked.

She lost both of her legs.

Her right arm was hurt.

2003
Iraq War
begins

2004
badly injured in
the Iraq War

1968    1984    1990    1993

a U.S. Army Black
Hawk helicopter

# Helping Veterans

Tammy was in the hospital
for a year. Then she wanted
to help veterans. She tried
to get them better health care.
She worked to get them more jobs.

In 2006 Tammy ran

for U.S. Congress. She lost.

But the race was close. She still

worked to help veterans.

2006
loses race for
U.S. Congress

2006–2009
is Director of the
Illinois Department
of Veterans' Affairs

1968    1984    1990    1993    2003    2004

Tammy got a new job in 2009. Now she helped veterans around the country. She helped more young veterans. She worked to help homeless veterans.

2009–2011
works for the
U.S. Department of
Veterans Affairs

1968    1984    1990    1993    2003    2004    2006

# Work in Congress

In 2012 Tammy ran for
Congress again. This time
she won. She helped make
new laws for the country.

2012
elected to
U.S. Congress

1968    1984    1990    1993    2003    2004    2006    2009    2011

Tammy ran for U.S. Senate in 2016. She won. Only two other Asian-American women have been in the U.S. Senate. Tammy still works to help veterans.

2016
elected to
U.S. Senate

# Glossary

**army**—a group of soldiers trained to fight on land

**congress**—the elected government body of the United States that makes laws; Congress includes the Senate and the House of Representatives

**law**—a rule made by the government that must be obeyed

**military**—the armed forces of a state or country

**ROTC**—a program that teaches its members military leadership skills while they attend college; ROTC stands for Reserve Officers' Training Corps

**senate**—one of the two houses of U.S. Congress that makes laws

**unit**—a group of soldiers

**veteran**—a person who served in the armed forces

# Read More

**Ferguson, Melissa**. *U.S. Government: What You Need to Know*. Fact Files. North Mankato, Minn.: Capstone, 2018.

**Rodgers, Kelly**. *Remembering Our Heroes: Veterans Day*. Huntington Beach, Calif.: Teacher Created Materials, 2015.

**Westmark, Jon**. *The Iraq War: 12 Things to Know*. America at War. Mankato, Minn.: 12-Story Library, 2017.

# Internet Sites

Use FactHound to find Internet Sites related to this book.

Visit *www.facthound.com*

Just type in 9781515799559 and go.

Super-cool stuff!

Check out projects, games and lots more at
**www.capstonekids.com**

# Critical Thinking Questions

1. Why do you think Tammy wanted to do so much to help other veterans?
2. Name two ways Tammy worked to help veterans.
3. Describe a time Tammy did not give up on getting what she wanted.

# Index